Volume Two

FEET

D1520281

BIRD·CARVING Basics

Volume Two

FEET

Curtis J. Badger

STACKPOLE BOOKS

Published by
STACKPOLE BOOKS
Cameron and Kelker Streets
P.O. Box 1831
Harrisburg, PA 17105

Printed in the United States of America

10 9 8 7 6 5 4 3 2 1

First Edition

Cover design by Tracy Patterson

Interior design by Marcia Lee Dobbs

Cover photo: Goldeneye drake carved by Pat Godin.
Photographed by Dan Williams, reprinted with
permission from *Wildfowl Carving & Collecting*
magazine.

Library of Congress Cataloging-in-Publication Data

Badger, Curtis J.
    Bird carving basics / by Curtis J. Badger.
        p.   cm.
    Contents: Vol. 2. Feet.
    ISBN 0–8117–2338–0
    1. Wood-carving.   2. Birds in art.   I. Title.
TT199.7.B33   1990
731.4'62—dc20
                                            90–9491
                                            CIP

Contents

Acknowledgments

Dan Brown feels a certain amount of frustration that when he began bird carving some thirty years ago there were no how-to books such as this one to point him along the way. Perhaps for that reason, Dan has become known not only as an outstanding carver but as a gifted teacher as well. One of the finer traditions of bird carving is that carvers give freely of their experience and knowledge. Those who learned essentially on their own seem genuinely pleased to help less experienced carvers avoid the pitfalls they encountered. Dan, for example, has taught countless workshops, written magazine articles and book chapters, and appeared on more public programs than he cares to count.

Young carvers such as Larry Tawes, Jr., and Jo Craemer carry on the tradition, sharing carving techniques and shortcuts. The irony is that carving is a full-time profession for all three of these artists, and to an extent they are competitors, at least for the attention of collectors, but all three are friends and admirers of one another's work. In fact, it was Dan who suggested that Larry be included in this book. If there are professional jealousies and secrets, they were not apparent among this trio.

Such openness and generosity make it a pleasure to write about wildfowl artists, and I want to express my gratitude to Dan, Larry, and Jo for their help and for their patience in having my camera peeking over their shoulders as they did some very exacting work.

If you learn a few things from these three outstanding artists, do them a favor and pass along some of your expertise to another carver who is just starting out. It's a tradition these three carvers have followed well, and one I'm sure they would like continued.

Introduction

Paradoxically, bird carving in America is seen as the most conservative of arts. Indeed, in some quarters the genre is considered so conservative it is not seen as an art at all. After all, is a bird not a symbol of all that is free and boundless? When we depict birds in art should our imaginations not soar on wings? Should we not leave behind the earthly things we cleave to?

Contemporary bird carving in America seems unfairly bound by two forces that both counter and complement each other. On one hand there is the tradition of wildfowl hunting that says the purpose of a carved bird is to suggest a species or an attitude, and nothing more. On the other hand is the peculiar fetish for detail preoccupying so many contemporary carvers. This would lead the casual observer of the wildfowl art scene to deduce that there are but two legitimate approaches to wildfowl art: the traditionalist's reverence for the hunting decoy as totem, and the contemporary carver's fixation on detail. But there is more to wildfowl art than this wide road that separates the minimalists from the super-realists.

Our contemporary passion for perfection, although it can seem rather mechanical and mindless, is not necessarily symptomatic of an art mired in detail for detail's sake. The bird has to be accurate, yes, but after it becomes accurate it has to soar; it has to express something timeless and enduring. Some contemporary bird carvings end at accuracy, and they become no more than clever models. Others, when made by skilled hands and an eye that knows birds, are able to transcend the obvious and become not just a single bird, but something that represents all birds.

Contemporary bird carving, it seems to me, has been mistakenly labeled as ultraconservative by the American public. Certainly there are some carvers for whom detail is an end in itself, but contemporary wild-fowl art runs the gamut from impressionism to realism, and techniques are as varied as are the men and women who employ them.

One of the objectives of this series is to demonstrate that in art there is no right or wrong, only different solutions to the same problem. This volume deals with the very pedestrian subject of feet, but when we examine in detail how three very different artists go about creating feet, we see a variety that demonstrates genuine resourcefulness and creativity. Just as the completed birds of Larry Tawes, Jr., Dan Brown, and Jo Craemer differ in style and substance, so too do their techniques differ.

Dan began carving around the time Larry was born, and his method clings more closely to the traditions of bird carving; that is, most of the process is done in wood. Larry, however, believes that a modern synthetic material, two-part epoxy, can more closely approximate the texture and tone of the skin of waterfowl. Jo, who began carving in the early 1980s after a career as a Navy nurse, uses a variety of techniques and materials, ranging from wood to metal to epoxy.

Each of the methods discussed in this book is perfect—for the carver who is using it. Each has been fine tuned over years of work, and each serves the motives and objectives of the carver. While Dan admires Larry's synthetic tree duck feet, the process might not be right for Dan's particular style of carving. And vice versa.

The goal, then, is to borrow what you can from these talented artists, and to distill and amplify their methods until they match your own personal goals. The idea is not to copy the techniques of Dan, Larry, or Jo, but to use their approaches as a jumping-off point for your own voyage of self-discovery. After all, that's what creativity is all about.

1
Larry Tawes, Jr.
Making a Foot for a Tree Duck

For Larry Tawes, Jr., a thirty-three-year-old carver from Salisbury, Maryland, two-part epoxy is the perfect material for making waterfowl feet. Epoxy is readily available at hardware and plumbing supply stores, it's fairly easy to work with, and its texture and pliability produce a very lifelike replication of a waterfowl foot.

Larry got interested in bird carving in 1970. His father, after spending some time studying with the well known carvers Steve and Lemuel Ward of Crisfield, Maryland, became interested in the art, and Larry, Jr., followed. "It was a typical father-son thing, I guess," Larry says. "He got interested in carving, and what he did, I wanted to do."

Both of the Taweses began carving as a hobby, and they slowly began to sell birds as interest in carving began to increase in the 1970s. When Larry grew up, he worked with his dad for eight years as a waterman on the Chesapeake Bay and for several more years in the masonry business. In the late 1970s Larry, Sr., decided to devote full time to bird carving, and shortly thereafter Larry, Jr., did also.

Larry, Jr., like his dad, started by making gunning birds. His grandfather was a Crisfield native and the tradition of waterfowl hunting and hunting decoys was a part of Larry's life as he was growing up. But in the mid-1970s, when interest in decorative birds began to grow, Larry began searching for ways to make detailed, highly realistic carvings. As a result, he developed tools and techniques that fit his tastes and goals in carving. The use of epoxy, for example, is a technique Larry learned from a carver friend but has adapted to his own style, even creating a personal set of tools to work with the medium.

Larry today works in a comfortable studio just outside Salisbury. A pond and an aviary are in his back yard, providing constant opportunities to study every nuance of waterfowl behavior.

The fulvous tree ducks Larry made in this session were entries in the World Class Decorative Lifesize category of the 1989 Ward World Championship. Before carving, Larry spent months studying a pair of tree ducks he kept in his aviary. There is no better way, he says, to capture not only the detail of a bird, but its spirit.

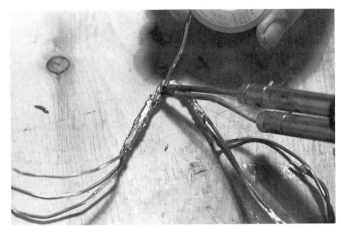

Larry begins the foot by using 12-2 copper wire to form an armature around which the epoxy foot will be shaped. Three pieces of wire are used, one for each toe, and the wires are twisted and soldered together.

Larry leaves an additional twelve inches of wire on the foot armature to serve as a handle during the shaping process. The toes are then measured and cut to length, and the joints, or knuckles, are created by bending the wire. Larry does this from memory, but beginning carvers might want to use a cast study foot as a reference.

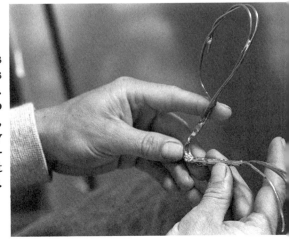

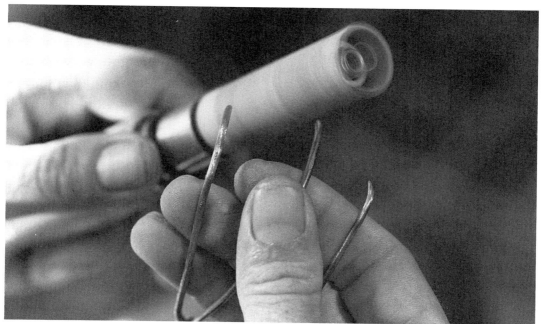

Before mixing the epoxy Larry uses a grinder to shape each of the three toenails. He also uses the grinder to smooth solder joints and to remove solder flux. The metal armature is then cleaned with lacquer thinner before the epoxy is applied.

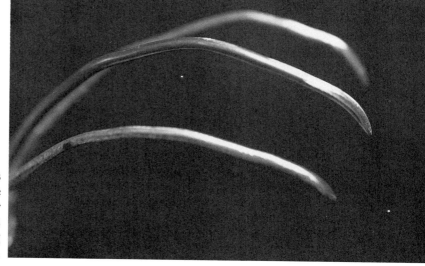

The foot armature is now properly shaped, the nails are in the proper position, and Larry is ready to begin applying the epoxy.

Larry uses two-part epoxy available at hardware
stores and plumbing-supply businesses.

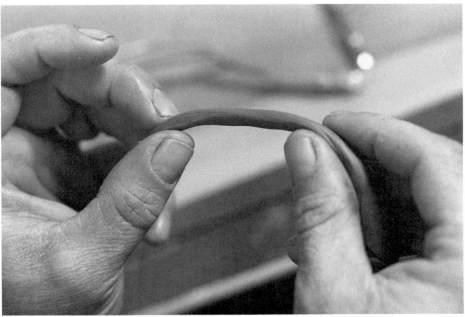

Larry rolls out the epoxy in the general shape of
the toe. He makes the toe slightly longer than necessary; any surplus will be cut off later.

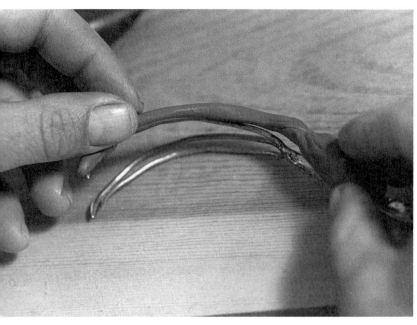

The rolled epoxy is placed on top of the wire and is pressed down so the wire enters the epoxy. Be sure to leave the raised "knuckles" in the wire, so the joints will be visible after the epoxy goes on.

As Larry works with the epoxy he moistens his fingers with paint thinner to prevent the epoxy from sticking. Your fingers must be very clean when doing this.

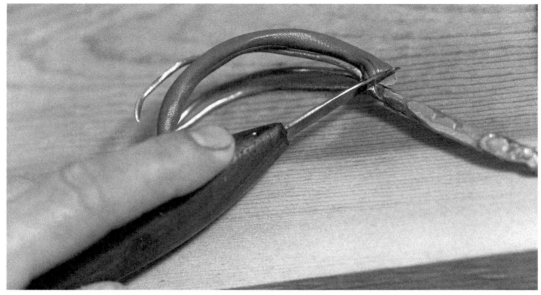

Larry uses a knife to trim excess epoxy from the toe. The cut should be made at the joint where the three wire "toes" join the leg.

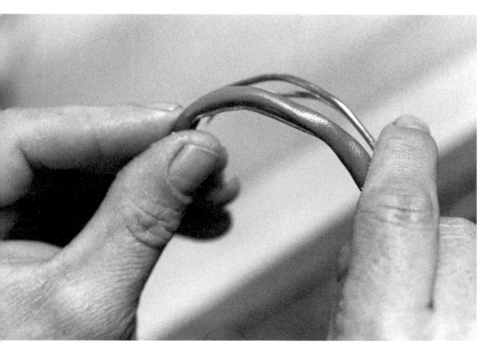

The epoxy is rolled over the wire and is shaped by hand. Be sure that the epoxy covers the wire armature completely.

Larry uses his fingers, moistened with paint thinner, to smooth and shape the epoxy toe. Note that a small flap, or web, has been left on the outside of the upper part of the toe.

Before detailing begins, the second toe is added in the same manner as the first toe. The two toes will be detailed simultaneously, and they will be prepared to accept the epoxy webbing, which will be added after the toes are detailed.

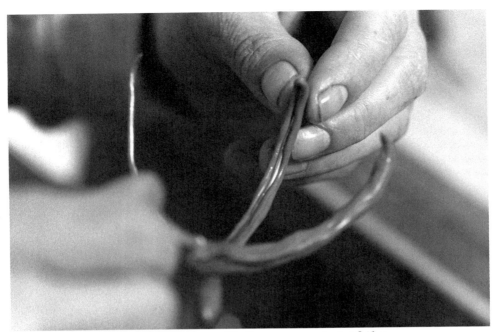

Here Larry places the rolled epoxy on top of the toe and presses it down onto the wire.

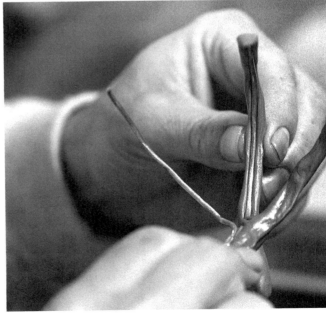

The epoxy, once the catalyst is mixed, will very soon become tacky. Larry retards the curing process by coating the material with paint thinner. Here he has moistened the epoxy with thinner and is rolling and pressing it around the copper armature.

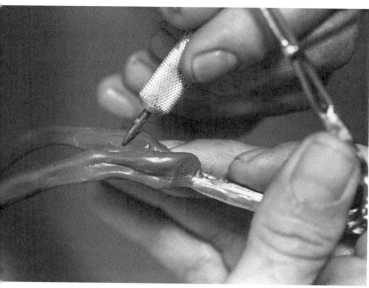

Now Larry is ready to add detail to the toes. He uses several tools, all of which he made himself. This tool originally was a small screwdriver, with the blade ground to form a blunt point. He uses paint thinner on the tools to prevent the epoxy from sticking.

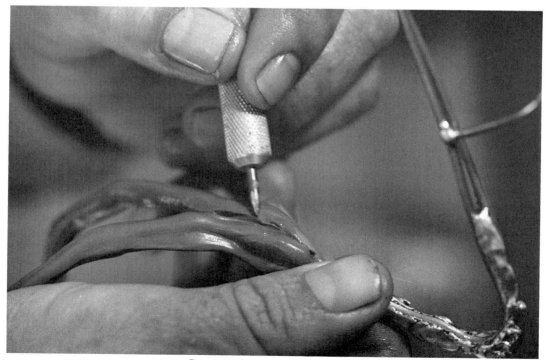

Larry also uses the "wrinkling tool" to shape the base where the two toes meet.

The opposite end of Larry's wrinkling tool is used to place a shallow groove onto the inside of each of the two toes. These grooves will later accept the epoxy webbing of the foot.

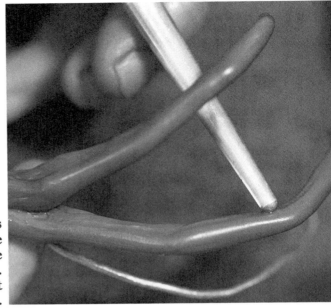

To make a tool similar to this, cut a piece of ³/₈-inch solid rod six to eight inches long and grind an end to create a blunt point. Polish with 320-grit sandpaper. Keep the tool moistened with paint thinner while shaping the epoxy. Note in this photo that the groove is not deep; it simply creates a shallow shelf onto which the webbing is placed.

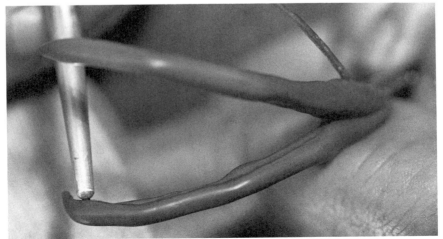

Larry is ready to detail the foot. Note that the toes are wider apart than they normally would be. The toes are separated to make installation of the webbing easier and to create a more realistic looking web. After the toes have been detailed and the webbing added, they will then be closed, creating realistic wrinkles and folds in the web. Larry begins detailing at the toenail, using a curved blade.

After the toenail is detailed, he uses the curved knife to define the scales on the top and sides of the toe. Larry creates the scales in three steps: A groove is pressed into the right side, then the left, and then onto the top. The curved knife approximates the shape of the scale and is easier to use than a straight knife.

Note how Larry presses the curved blade into the side of the left toe. Always have the curves going in the same direction.

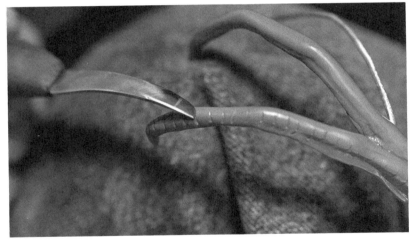

The scales are completed by pressing the blade onto the top of the toe, connecting the grooves on the left and right sides.

If the detail is too specific, too blatant, it won't be realistic, so Larry again moistens his finger with thinner and gently rubs out some of the detail, making it more subtle.

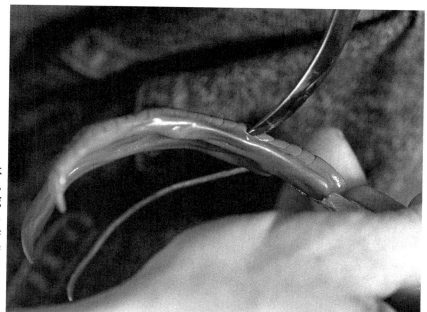

As you work with the foot, handling the soft epoxy, some of the detail may be lost. Use the curved blade to reinforce scales and detail.

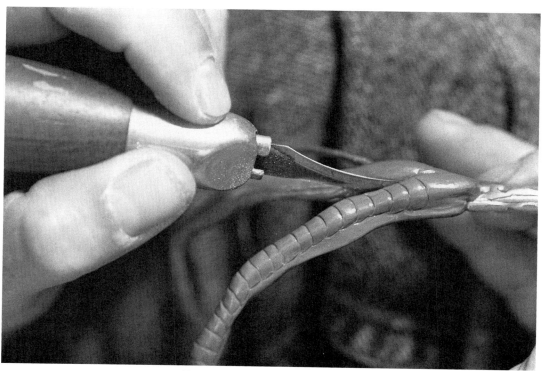

Larry uses a knife with a hook blade to shape the area between the toes.

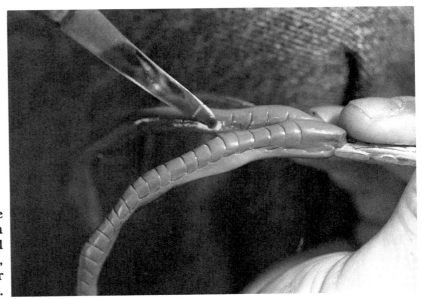

The curved blade is used again to create a small web, or shelf, on the under part of the toe.

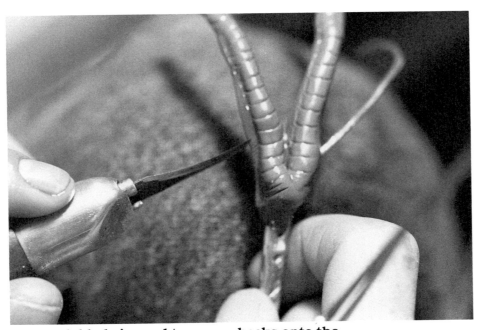

The hook blade is used to carve checks onto the small webbing on the outside of the toe. The blade is a standard hook shape, but Larry has sharpened both sides to make it more versatile.

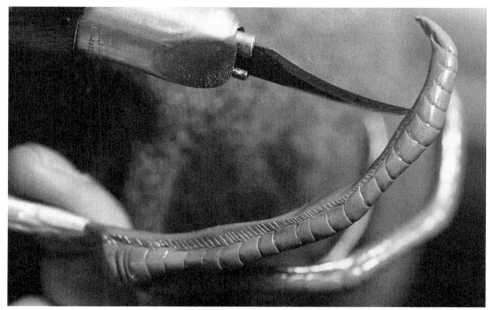

This detailing step is done much like checkering a gunstock, says Larry. The curved blade works better on the epoxy than a straight blade because it has less tendency to pull or tear the material. In this photo all the detailing cuts have been made in the same direction, but a crosshatch pattern will soon be added.

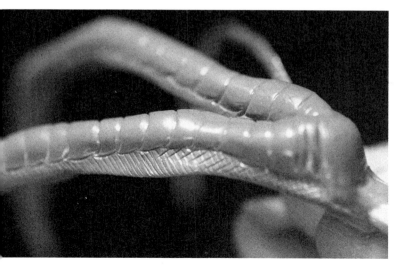

This close-up shows the "gunstock" checkering halfway completed on the left toe.

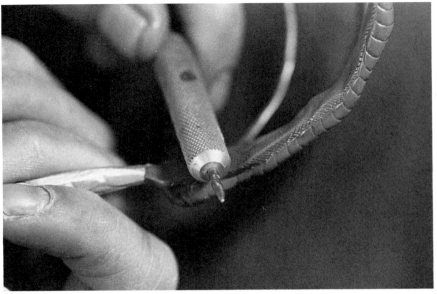

The checkered collet on this tool holder makes a perfect detailer for adding subtle checkering to the bottom of the foot.

When the checkering is completed, it looks like this. Now the web can be added. Larry will open up the toes to an angle of about fifty degrees to make insertion of the webbing easier.

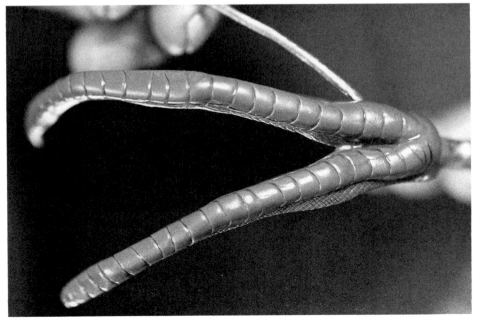

You have to be very careful at this point, says Larry, because the epoxy is very sticky and can attract dirt and dust particles. Use thinner to clean your hands before handling it.

Another batch of epoxy is mixed and is rolled out to form a flat sheet. A miniature dough roller would work great, says Larry, but he usually flattens the epoxy by hand. Use thinner to prevent the epoxy from sticking to hands or tools. Use small scissors to cut the webbing to approximate size and shape.

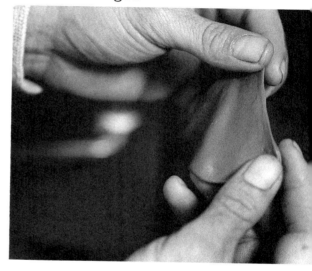

Larry shapes the web by hand, making it slightly larger than necessary. Excess will be trimmed off later.

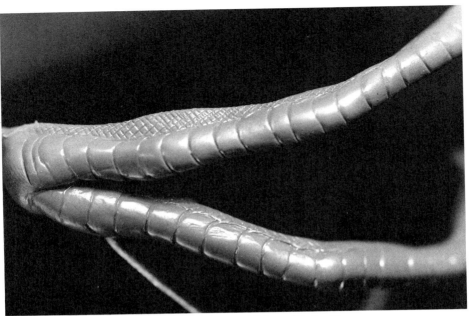

The toes are ready to accept the webbing. Note the
shallow shelf on the inside of the middle toe,
where the scales are separated from the checkering on the bottom. The web should adhere at
this point.

Larry cuts the
web to shape
and inserts
it between the
toes. The
web and the
toes will adhere
on contact, so
be careful when
positioning
the web.

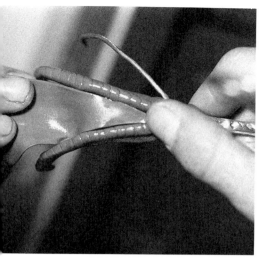

Larry usually starts at the rear of the toes and tries to apply the webbing to one side at a time.

Larry keeps his fingers moistened with thinner to prevent the epoxy from sticking. He uses no tools at this point, but instead gently guides the webbing into position with his fingers.

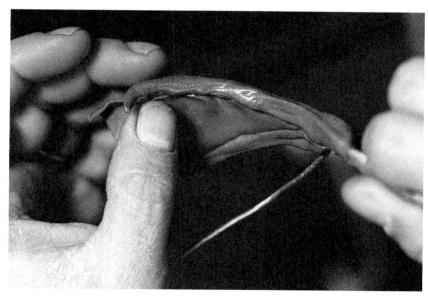

He uses his thumb to press the webbing into position on the lower part of the foot. The edge of the web should fit into the groove earlier pressed into the sides of the toes.

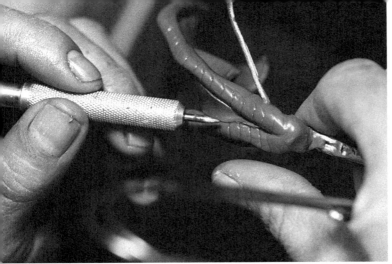

The wrinkling tool, moistened with thinner, is used to press the web into place on the top of the foot.

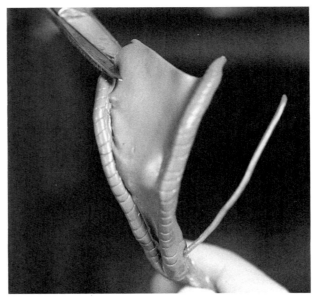

Once the web has been inserted and has adhered to the toes, excess can be trimmed off with small scissors moistened with thinner.

Larry uses his fingers to taper the edge of the web, approximating the thickness of an actual duck's foot.

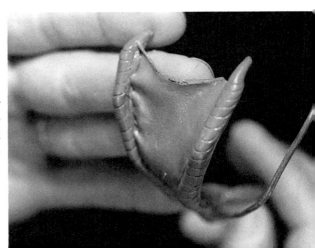

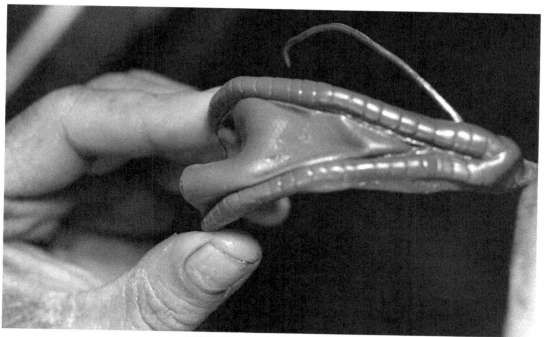

With the webbing inserted, Larry pulls the toes
together, creating realistic folds in the web.

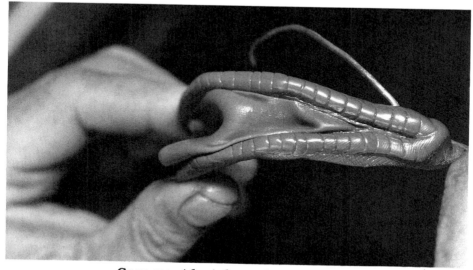

Care must be taken when doing this not to
obliterate detail on the toes or allow the webbing
to stick to itself.

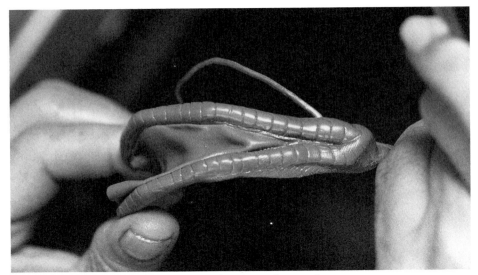

The amount of span between the toes depends on the posture of the duck. With its foot lifted, as this one will be, the toes would be fairly close together. If the duck were standing and had its weight on its foot, the toes would be farther apart. Always begin making the foot with the toes apart forty-five or fifty degrees, then close them after the webbing has been added. The webbing will be very pliable when first attached. Wait about twenty minutes before detailing the web to allow the epoxy time to harden slightly.

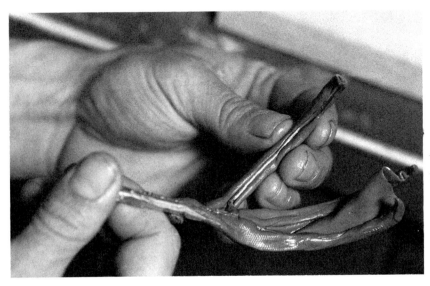

With the first web inserted, Larry begins the third toe just as he did the first two. A dab of epoxy is rolled out and is pressed over the wire armature and rolled onto it.

The toe is shaped by hand, and its base is joined to the base of the first two toes. If the epoxy on the first two toes has become too tacky to work with, use a brush to apply a light coat of thinner. This will restore some of the pliability of the medium.

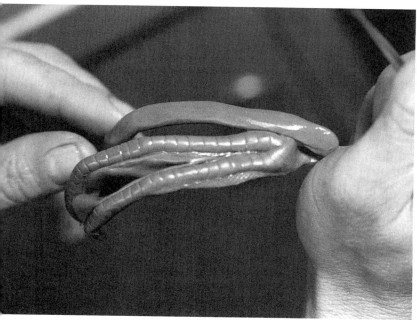

The toe is slightly thicker and larger than it will be when finished. The toe is shaped from the base toward the nail, with excess epoxy pulled toward the nail.

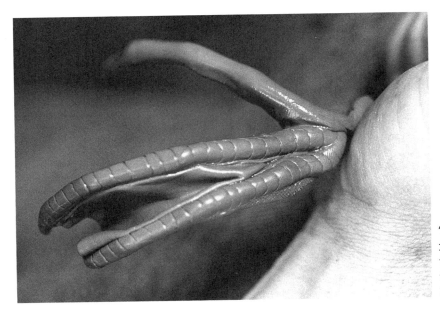

The base of the foot, showing the unfinished third toe, looks like this.

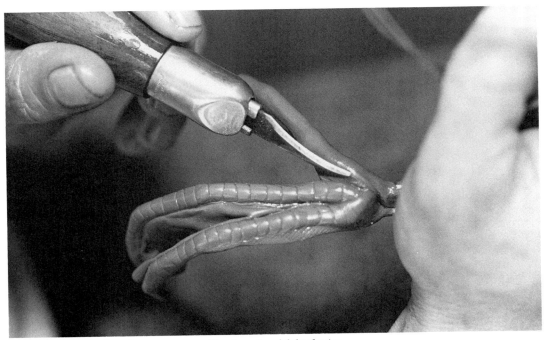

As he did earlier, Larry uses the hooked blade to shape the separation between the toes.

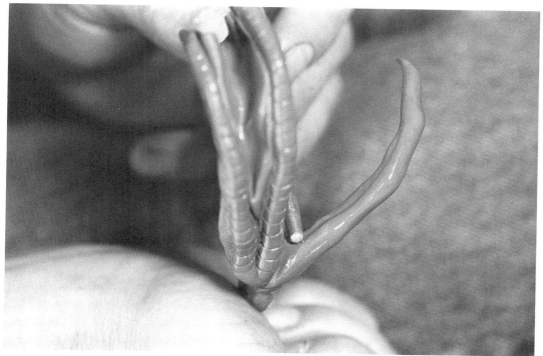

The blunt tool is used to form a crease along the bottom edge of the toe into which the web will be inserted.

Although the first two toes have been closed, keep the third toe separated from the middle toe to make detailing and insertion of the web easier.

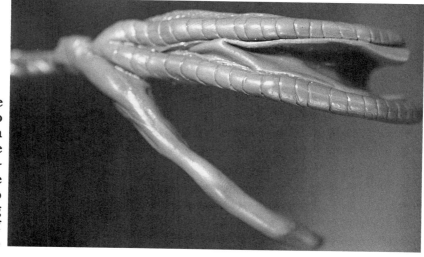

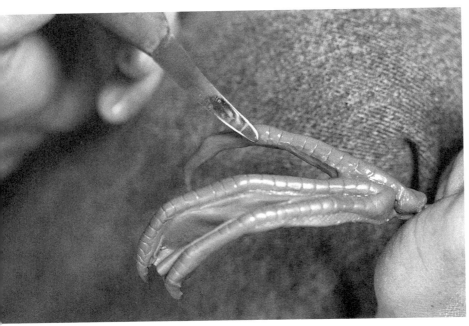

As on the first two toes, the curved blade is used to create scales. Grooves are cut on the sides of the toe, and then are joined by a groove cut into the top of the toe.

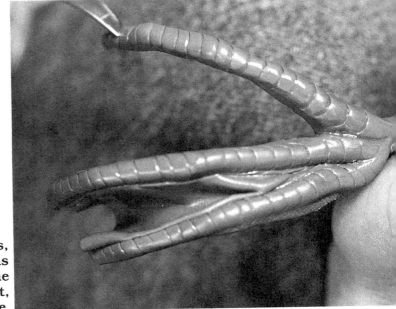

When cutting in scales, Larry usually begins at the claw and does the left and right sides first, then the top of the toe.

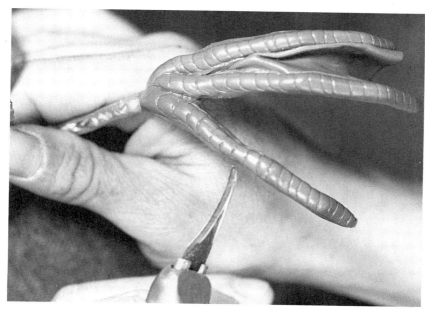

The scales have been completed; now Larry is ready to detail the bottom and side of the toe. For this, he will use the hook blade, cutting a crosshatch pattern as he did before.

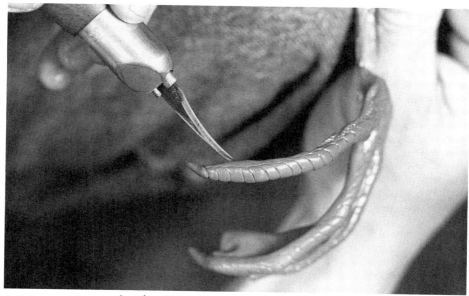

Again, the procedure is like checkering a gunstock. Lines are inscribed at an angle on one side of the toe, and then they are covered with a crosshatch pattern. Remember, good detailing is done with clean tools. Clean your tools often with thinner, and dip knife blades in thinner to prevent the epoxy from sticking.

Again, the collet of the tool is used to press a checkered pattern onto the bottom of the foot.

Most of Larry's tools are either found objects such as this, or handmade blades and styluses he has designed for his particular procedures.

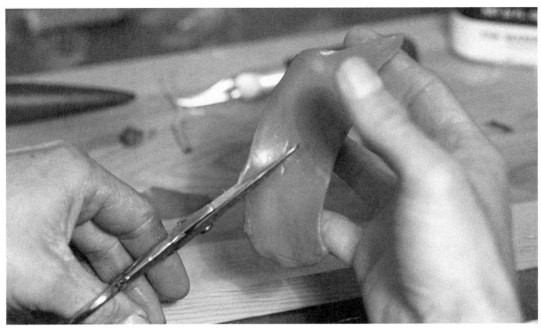

As he did earlier, Larry cuts the second web to approximate size. It can be slightly longer than necessary because excess can be trimmed off.

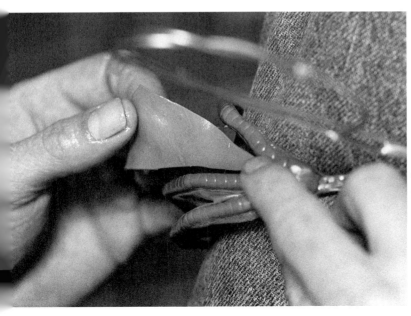

The pie-shaped web is inserted between the toes, adhering to them along the groove inscribed earlier with the blunt tool.

It's easier to attach the web first to one toe, then to the other. Because the epoxy forming the middle toe has partially cured, Larry will wipe it with thinner to increase its ability to adhere. The thinner retards the curing process and allows the epoxy to be worked for a longer period of time.

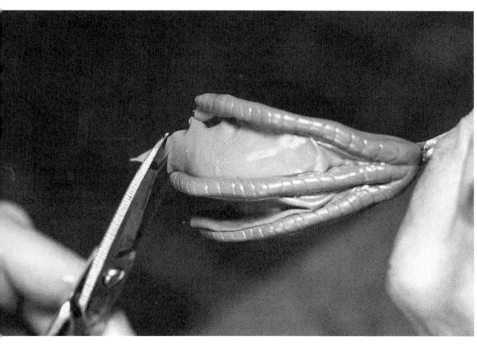

As he did before, Larry trims the outside of the web to size with a small pair of scissors, then uses his fingers to taper the edge of the web.

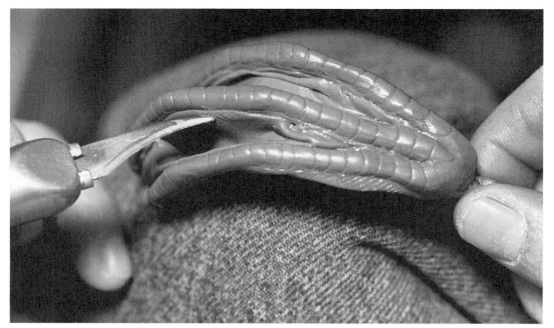

The third toe is closed, creating realistic folds in the web. The hook blade is used to press the web into shape and to create crosshatch detailing. Larry recommends waiting twenty minutes to let the epoxy cure slightly before detailing.

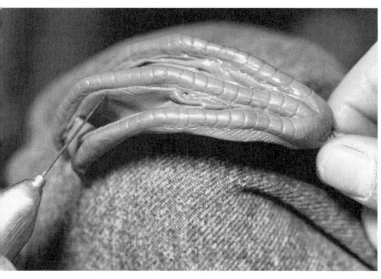

Note the pattern of detailing on the web. When working with epoxy, Larry prefers using a knife with a curved blade for detailing.

Now Larry is ready to add the rear toenail to the foot. He uses 12-2 wire, approximately $5/8$-inch long, and solders it into place at the base of the foot.

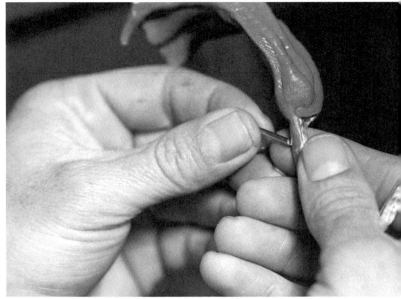

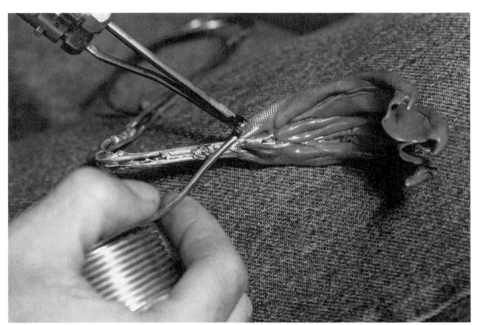

Larry waits until the foot is completed to add the nail, for two reasons. First, the nail would be in the way when working on the foot, and second, it would probably be broken off.

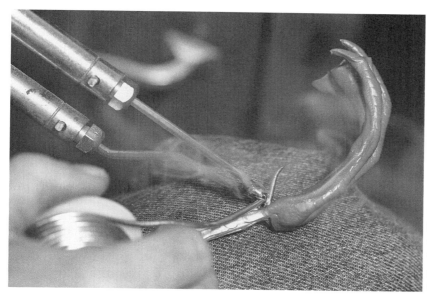

Care must be
taken when sol-
dering the
nail not to apply
excessive heat,
which
could damage
the epoxy.

With the toe soldered into position, Larry
uses a Dremel tool with 80-grit paper to clean the
joint. He washes the leg in thinner to remove
residue before applying more epoxy.

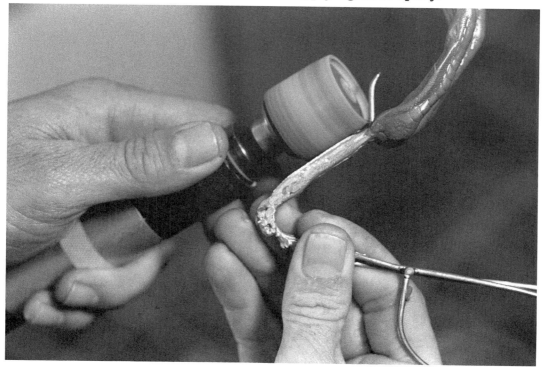

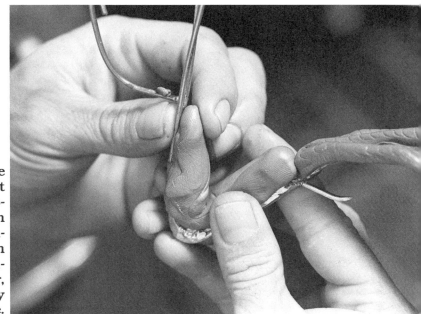

As he did with the toes, Larry rolls out a large bead of epoxy and places it on top of the wire armature of the leg. With his fingers lubricated with thinner, Larry rolls the epoxy around the wire.

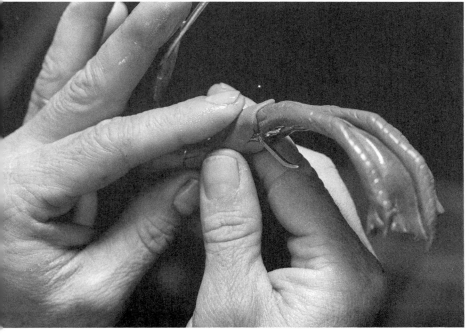

He uses his fingers to mold the epoxy into approximate shape, and to blend the new epoxy into the curing epoxy of the foot.

Here Larry shapes the knuckle at the ninety-degree bend. At this point he wants only to get the general shape of the leg. Muscle definition and detail will be added later.

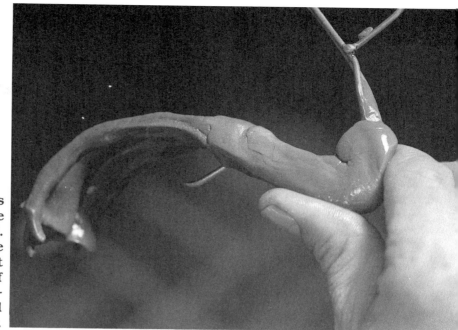

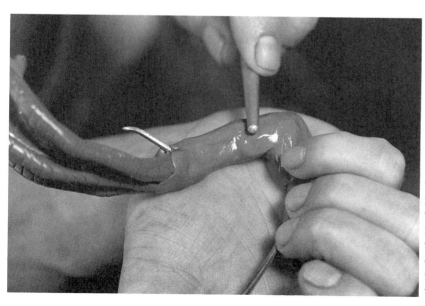

The shape is further defined with the metal stylus, which has been dipped into thinner to prevent sticking.

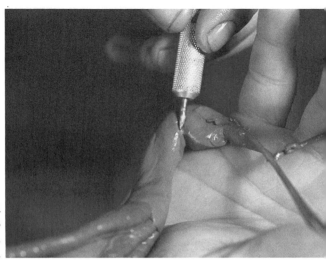

The sharper wrinkling tool is used to create the illusion of tendons in the leg. For reference material, try cast study feet or photographs.

Prior to detailing, Larry "slicks down" the leg and knuckle with thinner, and allows it to dry for about twenty minutes.

He begins detailing by using the curved knife blade to insert scales on the front of the leg. These are done in three steps, as they were on the toes.

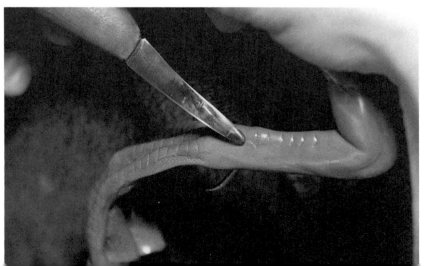

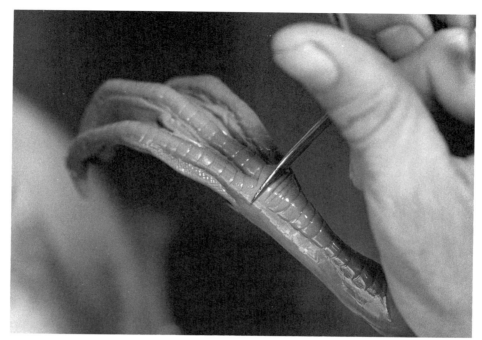

When the scales are done, Larry uses a straight knife to add wrinkles across the knee joint.

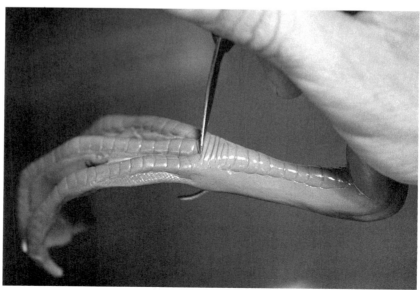

Note that the scales are curved, but the wrinkle lines are straight and are close together. If this detail is too obtrusive and "chickenlike," you can tone it down by wetting your finger with thinner and gently rubbing down some of the detail.

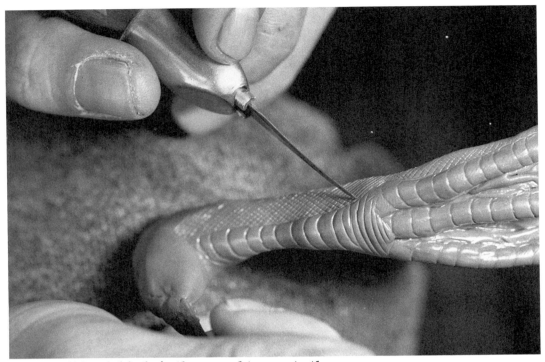

The small hook blade is then used to create the gunstocklike checkering on the bottom of the leg. Larry advises, "Don't pull the knife. Press it into the epoxy. If you pull the knife it will distort the epoxy."

Larry then uses the straight blade to carve wrinkles on the upper leg, just above the knee joint.

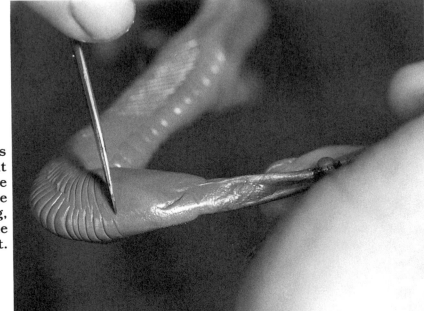

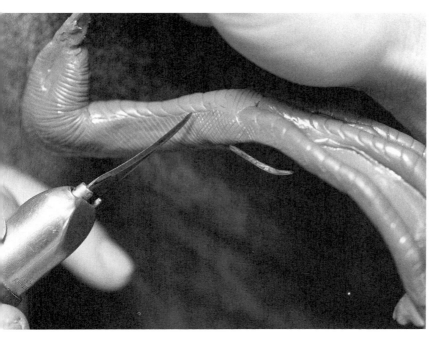

Wrinkles, scales, and checkering are almost completed. Now Larry must apply epoxy to the rear toenail.

A small dab of epoxy is used to create this nail. Care must be taken when applying it not to break the solder joint.

Roll out a small bead of epoxy and gently press it onto the wire.

Larry roughly shapes the nail with his fingers.

Larry uses the blunt stylus to blend the new epoxy of the nail into that of the leg, creating a smooth joint. Moisten the stylus in thinner to prevent sticking.

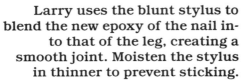

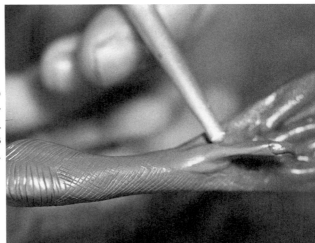

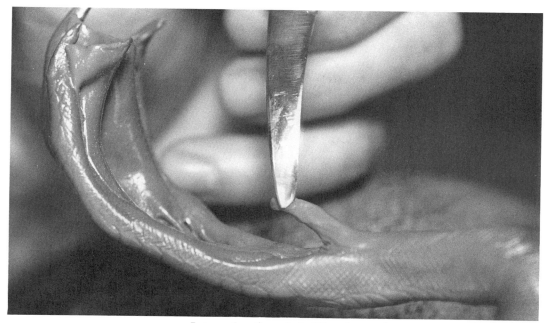

Larry begins detailing by using the curved blade to further refine the shape of the nail. Two small muscles on the sides of the nail are defined with this tool.

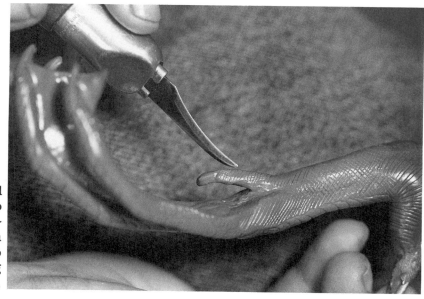

The hooked blade is used to create a cross-hatch pattern similar to that on the leg and toes.

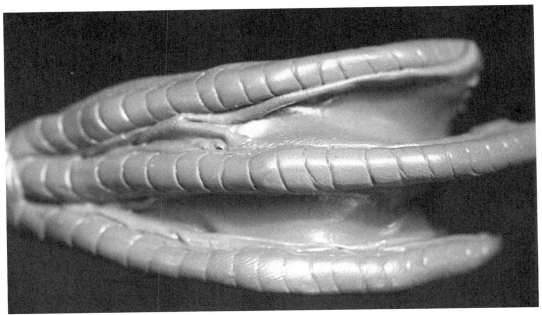

The completed foot, top view.

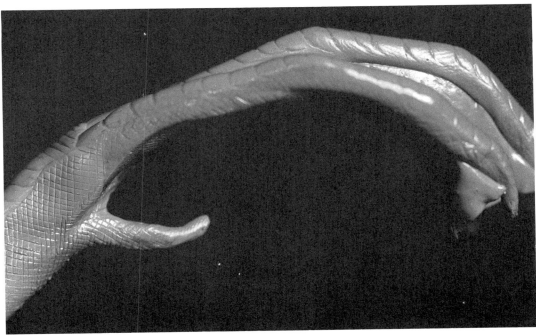

The completed foot, side view.

The completed foot, bottom view.

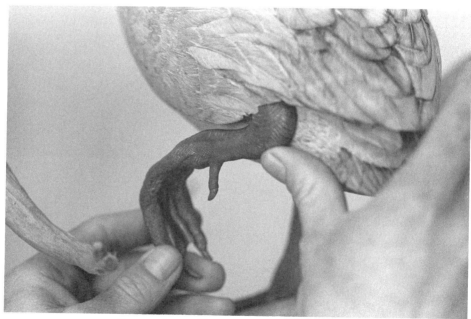

Larry has clipped off the excess wire "handle" and now inserts the leg into the body of the tree duck. Larry inserts the leg before the epoxy fully cures, but he covers the leg with a plastic material such as Saran Wrap before inserting it. This allows the leg to conform to the shape of the body, but the plastic prevents the epoxy from sticking to the wood. Later he will cement the leg in place.

With the feet inserted and the birds mounted on the bases, Larry is ready to begin painting.

The artist at work: Larry Tawes, Jr. of Salisbury, Maryland.

2
Dan Brown
Carving a Foot for a Standing Teal

When Dan Brown began carving birds thirty years ago, there were no how-to-carve books, no videotapes, no seminars with leading artists. So Dan learned to carve by "just doing it."

He was born in Dover, Delaware, grew up on the Nanticoke River in Maryland, and spent as much time waterfowl hunting as he could. So an interest in carving and collecting decoys came as an extension of hunting. "There were a lot of canvasbacks on the river in those days," he says. "I'd go out and find some old wooden canvasback decoys floating on the river and I'd bring them home. They weren't worth much then, but I liked them. I began collecting decoys before I realized I was collecting decoys."

In those days, some thirty years ago, you could buy a Ward Brothers decoy for $10 to $15, and you could buy Ira Hudsons for $5 to $6. Dan bought decoys to hunt with and to admire after the season had ended.

He began carving to make decoys for his own rig, and to repair some of his favorite hunting decoys. He visited Crisfield often, and soon came under the spell of Steve and Lem Ward, who carved masterful decoys in their small workshop.

"I played semipro baseball in Crisfield, and later I was there a lot as a salesman for Pet Milk. It got so every time I went to Crisfield I'd go see the Wards, and then it got so I'd not only go see them, but I'd spend the day there."

By the late 1960s Dan was finding a market for his birds; in 1968 he left his job and devoted full time to his carving, which by then had evolved from making working decoys to creating more intricate, detailed decorative carvings. "Lem always encouraged me to develop my own style and my own patterns," says Dan, "but my birds looked like his for a long time. I was so totally exposed to the Wards that when I made a bird I made it like theirs because I thought that was how a bird was supposed to look. But gradually I began to develop my own style and technique. There were no books on carving then, and if you wanted to carve you had to pick up a lot of it on your own. It took me years to get rid of a lot of bad habits."

Although there were frustrations in having to learn on his own, the lack of direction forced Dan to develop his own techniques, such as his method of making feet illustrated here. In this session he makes two feet for a carving of a green-winged teal pair mounted on a driftwood base. Dan uses a lead template as a guide in carving the foot for the standing drake. Then he carves a folded, raised foot for the hen. In this section he also demonstrates his method of carving toes and toenails from solder.

The position of the foot determines to a large extent how it will be carved. The foot that supports the weight of a bird, as seen in the first sequence, will be carved differently from a raised foot. Dan studies photos and videotapes of live birds before determining the design of the feet.

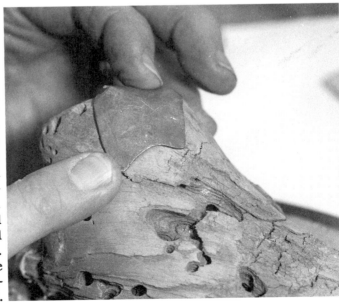

Once he decides where the bird will be located on the base, Dan begins by using a lead template to transfer the contour of the mounting surface to the foot. The soft lead is pressed into position, then the foot is carved to match the contour of the lead template. This is the right foot, and an "R" has been scratched into the surface of the lead. The opposite side of the template is the correct figuration for the left foot.

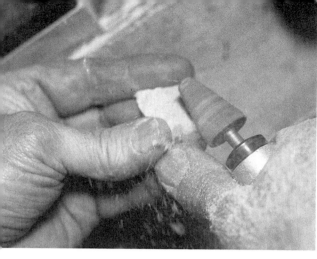

Dan begins by using a tapered Kutzall bit to shape the bottom of the block of wood so that it matches the contour of the lead template. "The template should actually fit into the bottom of the foot," he says. "That way you ensure that the bottom of the foot will fit on the base and look natural, as if the bird were gripping the wood."

A pencil is used to draw in the toes and define the web.

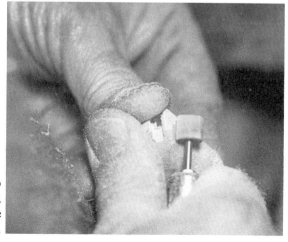

A cylindrical cutter is used to shape the outside of the foot. Dan has cut a notch at the rear of the foot where the foot will join the leg.

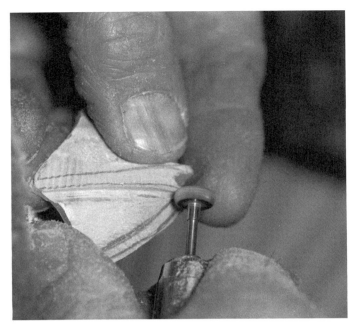

A cutter in the shape of a small wheel is used to cut down the webbing. The pencil marks establishing the high points of the toes are left as reference.

Dan uses another cutter to further reduce the thickness of the webbing. He prefers a high-speed grinder with a fine cutter for this procedure. "I prefer this tool to the Foredom for doing webbing," he says. "It's more stable and has less vibration and you can do finer work with it."

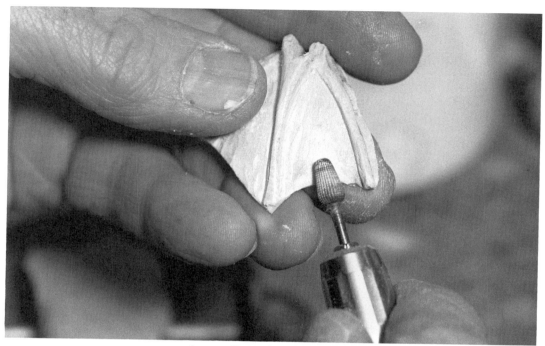

A small conical cutter is used to taper the edge of the web. "You don't have to make your webbing as thin as you might think," says Dan, "but you do have to make the edges thin to give the illusion of thinness." He uses the same cutter to shape the toes.

The foot has been shaped, but before Dan textures it he uses a burning pen to cut a small slot in the end of each toe, which will accept the toenail.

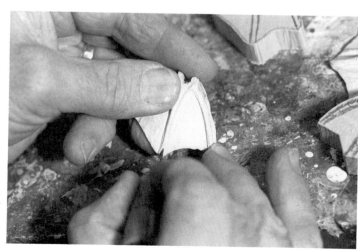

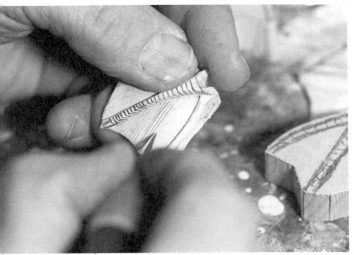

A burning pen is used to texture the foot. "It helps to have a lead study foot," says Dan. "A good study foot will show the texture of the webbing as well as the scales on the top of the toes." Note the slot left at the end of the middle toe where the nail will be inserted.

Dan textures the webbing in a crosshatch pattern that when painted will closely resemble the detail of a teal's foot.

After detail is burned onto the foot, Dan is ready to insert the toenails. He had earlier burned slots where the nail would be inserted. Now he uses a very narrow cutter on his high-speed drill to enlarge the slot.

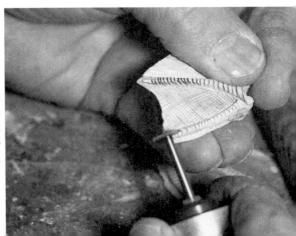

Toes carved from wood are far too fragile, Dan says, so he makes his out of solid-core (as opposed to acid-core or resin-core) solder. Solder is malleable, easy to carve, and it will take much more abuse than wood. He begins by snipping off a piece about 1/4-inch long, cutting it at an angle.

Dan uses a sharp knife to carve the nail. He uses a protector on his thumb to prevent cuts. After shaping the front of the nail, Dan will use a pair of small needle-nose pliers to crimp the back part, making it fit into the slot he cut into the toe.

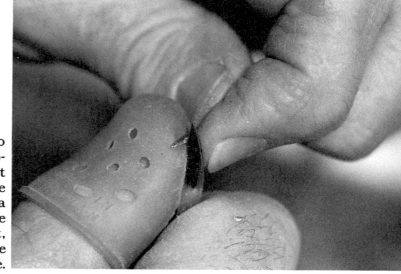

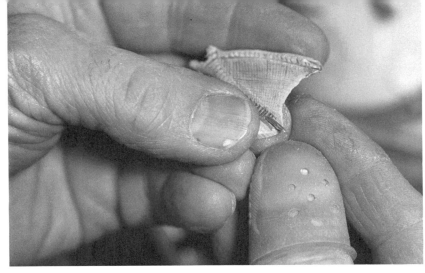

Dan glues the toenails into place with an adhesive such as Duco Cement. The nail is pressed into the slot that was earlier cut with the burning pen.

A slightly different procedure is used for carving the back toe. Dan cuts a piece of solder approximately one-half inch long and places it lengthwise in a vise. The vise is used to flatten an edge of the solder, creating the illusion of a small web. Place slightly less than one-half of the solder's diameter in the vise.

It's important to use a precision-made vise to crimp the solder accurately and cleanly. This one is a refugee from a machine shop, and was used with a drill press.

After the edge is crimped, the piece of solder should look like this. You'll have to experiment a few times to get the exact shape you need. Solder is very malleable and can be trimmed and shaped with a sharp knife. Be sure to leave enough of a stem on the toe so it can be inserted in the rear of the leg.

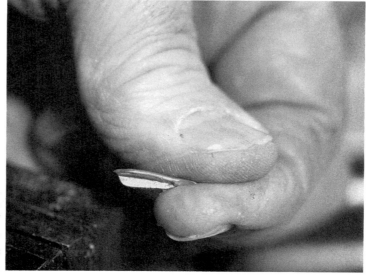

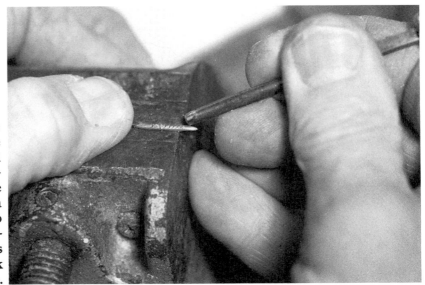

When Dan has the rear toe in the desired shape, he returns it to the vise and uses a U-gouge to create the illusion of scales along the back of the toe.

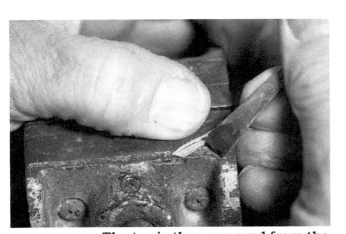

The toe is then removed from the vise and a small chisel is used to create a crosshatch pattern on both sides of the webbing.

The finished rear toe, with the nail carved and the webbing textured, looks like this. A stem about 1/8-inch long will be used to mount the toe on the leg.

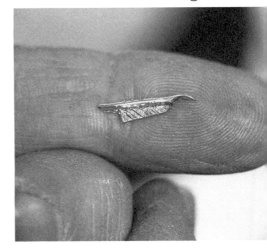

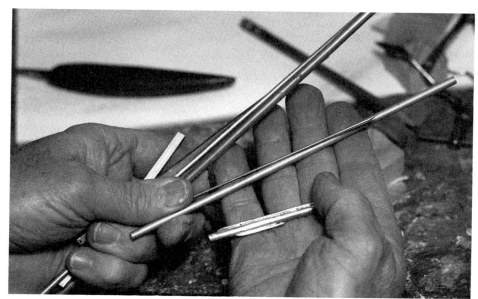

The leg of the standing teal is actually a brass tube. Dan's shop has an assortment of tubes in various sizes, and he'll pick one of the appropriate diameter for the species of bird he's working on. The cast study foot is a good reference for determining the length and diameter of the leg.

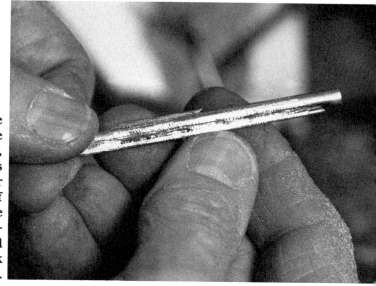

For the teal, Dan will use three different tubes. A large tube forms the main part of the leg, and Dan solders two small tubes on opposite sides. These smaller tubes will give the illusion of tendons in the leg. In effect, the brass tubes constitute a skeletal construction. The "skin" will be added by painting on a thick coat of synthetic wood filler.

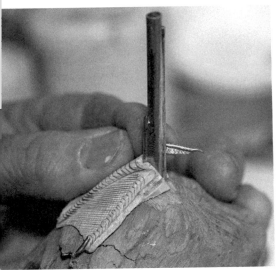

A hole is drilled in the base to accept the brass tube, and the foot is tried for fit.

Dan uses solvent to thin down a wood-base filler so it can be applied to the leg with a brush. Plastic Wood and similar fillers can be used, but Dan advises using a filler that has a wood base rather than a clay base. Thin down the filler just enough so you can apply it with the brush. You don't want it so thin that it will run down the leg.

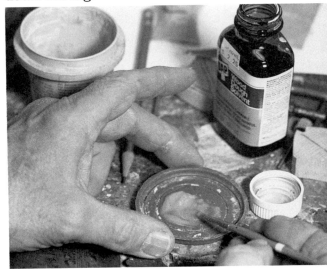

Dan covers the entire metal part of the tube that will show. The top of the tube will fit into the body of the bird, and filler will not be applied to it.

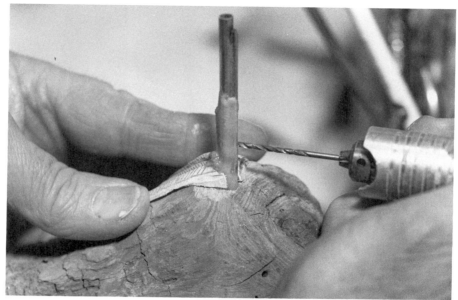

After the filler dries, Dan uses a small bit to drill a hole to accommodate the small rear toe of the bird. Again, a cast study foot is a good reference for establishing the exact location of the toe. Use a sharp punch to make an indentation at the location of the hole; otherwise the drill bit might drift off position.

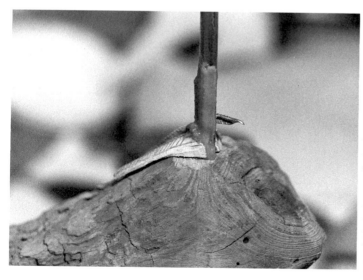

The foot now is glued to the base, the rear toe has been inserted and cemented into position, and the wood filler is drying. As soon as it hardens, Dan will use a burning pen to scribe texture lines onto the leg.

A close-up of the foot shows detail of the webbing and the scale marks on the tops of the toes. The three toenails have been inserted and cemented, and the foot is ready for paint.

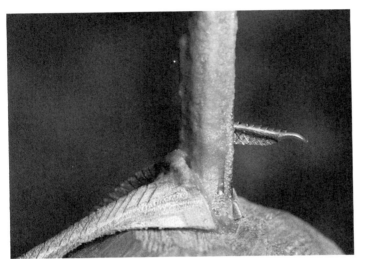

Notice the location of the rear toe and the folds of ''skin'' at the top of the foot. Dan will add more filler later to further refine the transition between foot and leg.

And now the leg is ready for detail. The burning pen is used on a low setting to scribe a fine crosshatch pattern onto the leg. When the texturing is complete, the leg will be ready for paint.

The finished standing foot looks like this. Note that Dan soldered a piece of square tubing onto the top of the leg. This prevents the bird from twisting once it is mounted onto the leg.

Another view
of the finished foot.

Dan begins the second foot by sketching it on a piece of paper. When he is satisfied with the position and appearance of the foot, he transfers the sketch onto a piece of wood, drawing the top and side patterns as shown here.

This close-up shows the detail and shape of the foot, which is now ready to be cut out.

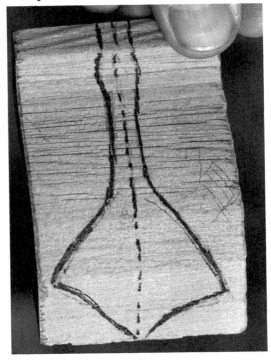

The side view is then cut out on a bandsaw or scroll saw, and Dan refines the top view, adding a center line and checking the shape of the foot against reference material.

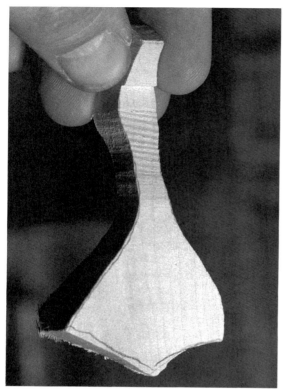

The roughed-out foot looks like this. Now Dan will sketch the toes and webbing onto the foot as he did earlier with the standing foot.

First Dan places the roughed-out foot into position on the teal, making sure that the bend of the leg looks natural.

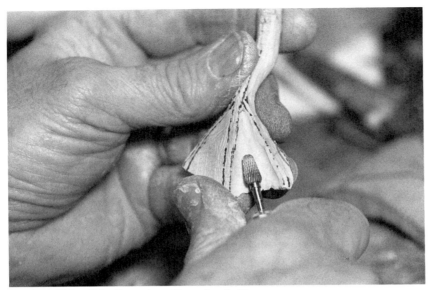

As he did with the standing foot, Dan uses a carbide cutter to remove wood along the webbing. The pen marks that define the toes will remain until the rough carving is complete. They serve as reference lines.

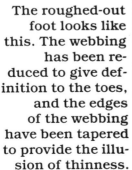
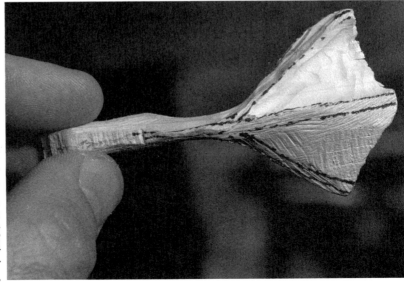

The roughed-out foot looks like this. The webbing has been reduced to give definition to the toes, and the edges of the webbing have been tapered to provide the illusion of thinness.

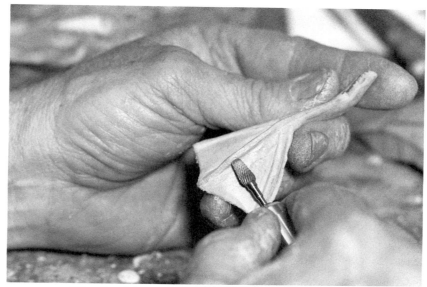

The foot is nearly shaped and ready for texture now. Unlike the standing foot, a brass armature will not be used with the lifted leg, so the leg section must be carved to provide the illusion of tendons. Dan uses a variety of bits. "The cutter to use is the cutter that works best for you," he says.

The leg tendons are now carved, and the foot is ready for texturing. "It helps a great deal to have a cast study foot or good photographs of a foot when you do this," says Dan.

Dan has carved the nails and inserted two of them, and is now using a burning pen to add detail to the webbing and toes. "This foot is very similar to the flat foot," he says, "the only difference is the position, and you have to do a little more planning."

Half of the webbing has been detailed with a crosshatch pattern, and detail on the toes has been scalloped with the pen, creating the illusion of scales.

This close-up of the foot shows the pattern Dan uses to burn detail into the foot. The nail on the right has been cemented in, but the one on the left has not yet been inserted. The groove where the nail will fit has been cut.

Dan's next step is to make the back toe and to insert it in the leg. The toe was made in a vise, as demonstrated earlier, and was cemented into the leg with Duco Cement. Notice the detail of the tendons and joint in the leg. A study foot is very helpful in creating such realistic detail.

A close-up shows detail of the back toe.

Before cementing
the foot into place,
Dan tries it
for fit and position.

The finished product. The nails have been completed and the foot has been inserted into the body of the bird and painted. The marks left by the burning pen, when painted, provide a remarkably realistic illusion of webbed feet.

3

Jo Craemer
Songbird Feet from Wood, Wire, and Epoxy

After twenty years as a U.S. Navy nurse, Jo Craemer is now sailing full speed into her second career as a bird carver. After retiring as a lieutenant commander in 1984, Jo and her husband moved to the coast of Delaware where they raise bird dogs, enjoy hunting and fishing, and in their spare time tend their fifty-acre farm. Jo's husband, a former Navy flier, now flies for Henson Aviation, and Jo spends most of her time either in her workshop or volunteering at the Ward Museum of Wildfowl Art in nearby Salisbury.

Jo began carving after attending the Mid-Atlantic Wildfowl Carving Exhibition while stationed in Virginia Beach in the early 1980s. She signed up for a course with world-class artist Lynn Forehand of Chesapeake, and from then on she was hooked on bird carving.

In recent years she has returned to the Mid-Atlantic as a competitor and has taken home a number of ribbons. In 1989 she entered the prestigious Ward Competition for the first time and won a third. Her goal now is to continue her rapid improvement and to compete at the top level of the art.

Jo credits her rapid rise to courses she has taken with such talented carvers as Forehand, Larry Barth, Bob Guge, Ernie Muehlmatt, and Bob Woodard. "Starting out with Lynn Forehand cut five years out of the learning process," she says. "I didn't have any bad habits. I didn't have any habits at all. What I learned from him in a few days would have taken me months or years on my own. All of my experience has been with these master carvers, and it has accelerated the learning curve tremendously. Now I'm concentrating on developing my own style, which comes with experience."

Jo specializes in songbirds and makes feet from either wood, wire, epoxy, or a combination. In this photo session she demonstrates two methods of making feet. In the first she carves toes from boxwood, an extremely hard, dense wood, and uses them in conjunction with epoxy and copper wire to make a foot and leg. In the second session she uses copper wire to make the toes, then covers all but the nail with epoxy. Each toe is then added to a copper and epoxy foot and leg. Jo uses cast study feet as a reference for size, position, and detail.

Jo begins the carving process by using a pencil to trace the outline of the toe from a cast meadowlark study foot. She uses either boxwood or holly, both of which are dense, hard woods that resist breakage, an advantage when carving a small, fragile songbird foot. The sections she uses here are cut on a radial saw from a length of wood measuring 2 by 1½ by 16 inches. She purchases the wood from Exin, Ltd., P.O. Box 1785, Greenville, SC 29602.

Once the outline is traced, Jo uses a Gesswein tool to rough out the toe. The length of the toe should be roughly parallel to the grain of the wood.

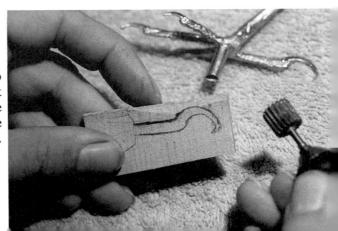

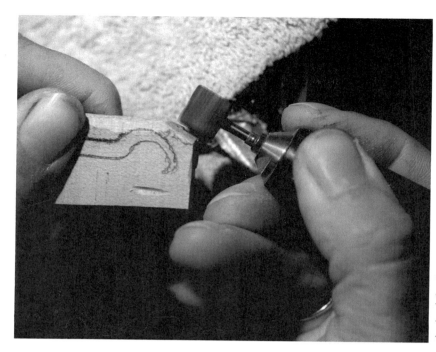

The large, squaring cutter on the Gesswein quickly removes excess wood. Jo will use finer bits to round the toe and then to add detail.

She leaves a large "handle" on the toe, which she grips with a small pair of needle-nose Vise-Grips. The pliers make the small toes easy to handle, reducing hand fatigue.

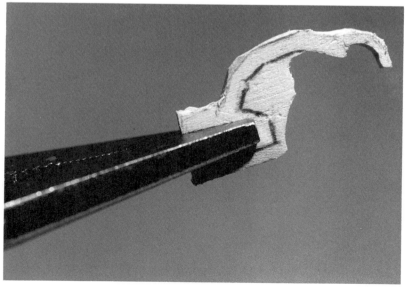

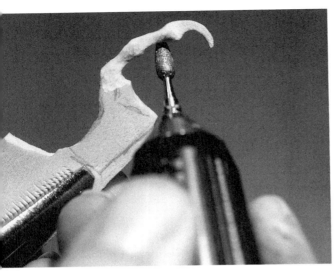

A flame-shaped ruby cutter is used on the Gesswein to round off the contours of the toe. The cast study foot is used as reference.

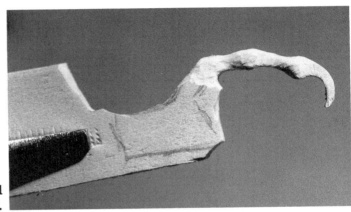

The toe is now rounded and is ready for detailing.

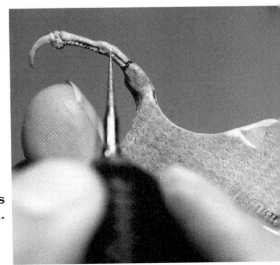

For this very meticulous step, Jo uses a fine diamond cutter on the Gesswein.

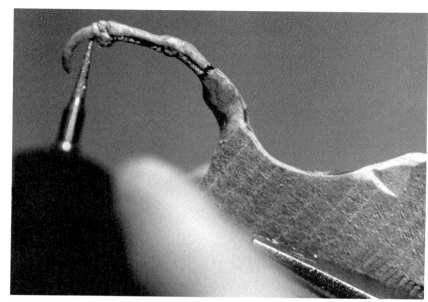

This bit is very sharp and care must be taken not to gouge the toe; a very light touch is required to render accurate detail.

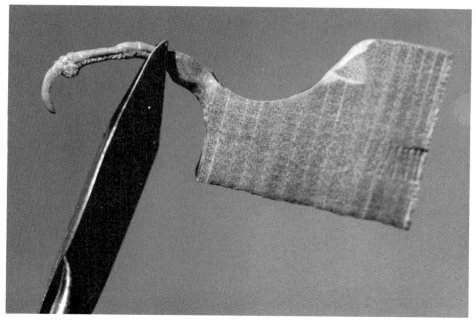

When the toe is completed, Jo uses small wire cutters to remove the toe from the wooden handle. Jo will repeat these steps for all four toes, using the study foot as a size reference.

A wooden dowel is used as a mount, and the leg and foot will be shaped on this, and then transferred to a branch of similar diameter when the bird is finished. A piece of 12-2 copper wire is inserted in a hole drilled into the dowel, and a dab of two-part plumbers' epoxy is placed around the bottom of the wire.

The wire will form the leg of the bird, and the epoxy will serve as the mounting medium for the wooden toes.

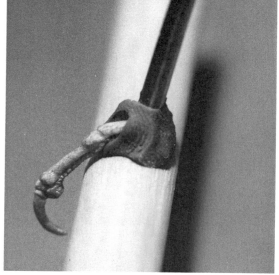

The first toe is pressed into the epoxy.

The second toe is added, and Jo uses a dental tool to detail the epoxy, which is beginning to harden.

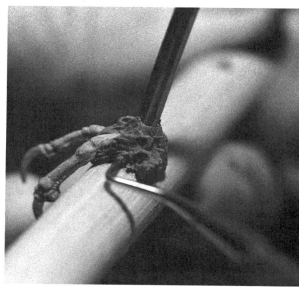

The other toes are added and the epoxy is smoothed and detailed.

More epoxy is added to the copper wire, and this becomes the leg of the bird. The epoxy is smoothed and detailed with dental tools. Again, use a study foot as reference for leg detail.

The finished downy, mounted on a dead limb.

A finished foot on one of Jo's downy woodpeckers. When painted, the wooden toes and epoxy/wire foot and leg blend nicely.

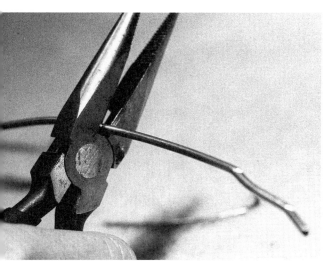

To make the second type of foot, Jo begins by clipping off about four inches of 12-2 copper wire. This will serve as the armature around which the foot will be built. Excess wire will be cut off later; leave enough to provide a convenient handle.

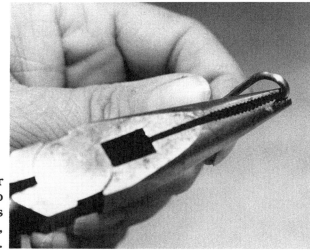

Her next step is to use a pair of needle-nose pliers to curve the end of the wire. This curve will serve as the nail, or claw, of the toe.

The curve should make a smooth, tight bend of about 180 degrees, as shown.

The wire then goes to an anvil, and a hammer is
used to flatten the curved claw portion of the toe.
The end of the claw should be tapered slightly.

The flattened wire looks like this. In the next few
steps the claw will be shaped with the Gesswein
tool.

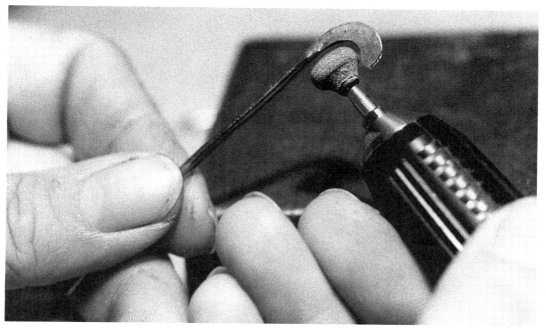

Jo uses a variety of bits to coax the copper into the proper shape. Basically, the procedure calls for sharpening the flattened wire into a claw-shaped point.

Any kind of metal-cutting stone will work. This shape provides the proper curvature of the claw.

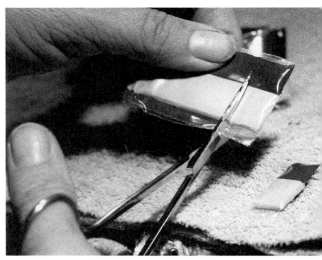

Once the claw is made, Jo uses two-part epoxy to create the fleshy part of the toe and foot. This is called ribbon epoxy, and it's available in most hardware and plumbing-supply stores.

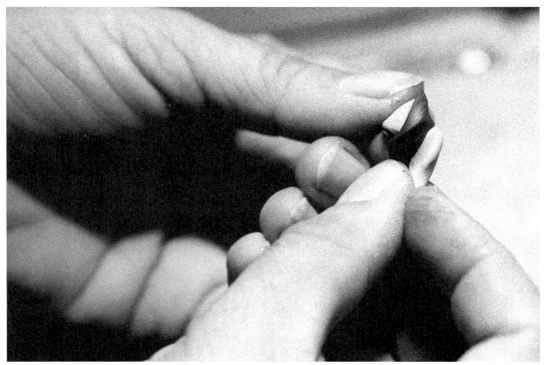

The two colors of the epoxy are mixed together by hand until they become a uniform shade of green. It's a good idea to cut out and discard the center strip of the epoxy ribbon where the two colors meet because the two chemicals have reacted and formed a rigid strip.

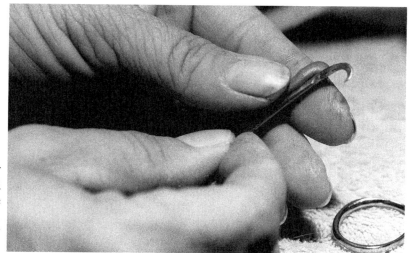

A bead of epoxy is rolled out and placed over the wire armature, leaving the claw exposed.

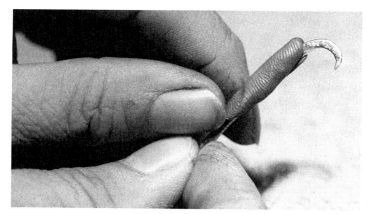

The epoxy is pressed down on the wire and worked over it until the wire is covered.

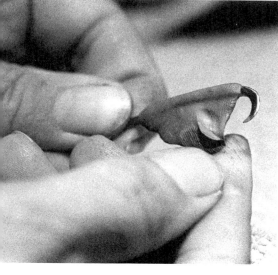

Jo leaves a flap of excess epoxy on the bottom of the toe.

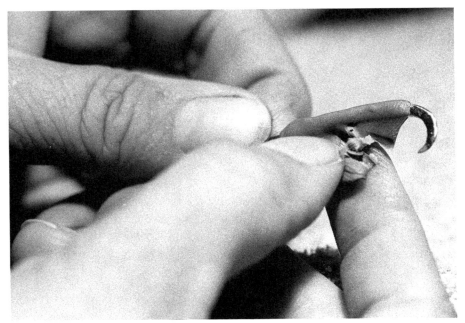

The excess epoxy is then torn away, leaving the correct amount of "flesh" on the toe. If in doubt, consult a study foot of the species you're carving.

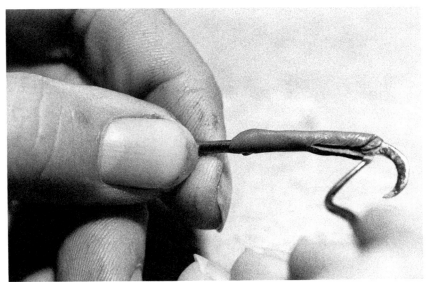

Once the epoxy is affixed to the wire, Jo uses dental tools to begin detailing the toe.

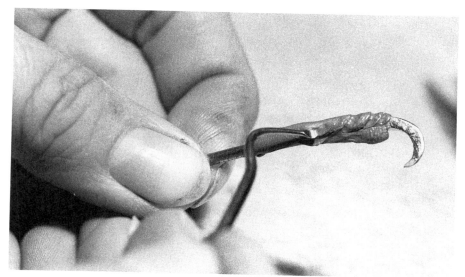

The idea is to create a series of overlapping scales along the toe. Jo begins at the claw and works up the foot. She has an extensive collection of dental tools, which work nicely with the epoxy. If the epoxy becomes sticky, Jo moistens the tool with alcohol or mineral oil.

This tool, also a refugee from the dentist's office, finishes the detailing of the toe. Jo repeats the process for all the toes before going on to make the foot and leg.

Wire cutters are used to remove the excess copper from each toe.

The foot and leg begin with another section of copper wire inserted in a wooden block. A dab of epoxy putty is placed at the bottom of the wire, and the toes will be inserted into this. You can make the leg and foot at any angle you desire.

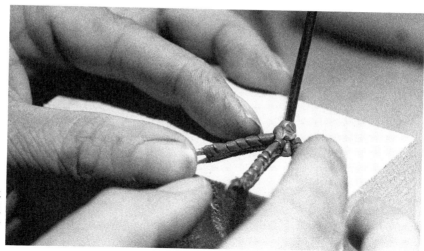

The three front toes are pressed into the epoxy joint.

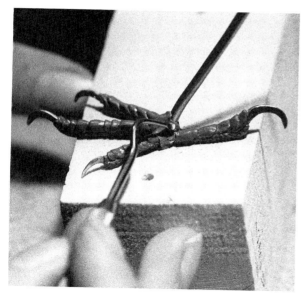

The back toe is added, and Jo uses another dental tool to smooth the junction between the toes and foot.

Another dab of epoxy is rolled out and is placed over the wire armature of the leg.

To ensure accuracy while detailing, Jo often refers to the cast study foot. When the detailing is finished, the foot is ready to be mounted onto the bird.

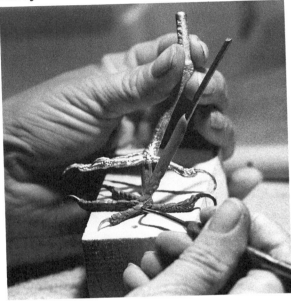

The dental tool is used to smooth the leg and add detail such as the illusion of tendons.

Jo Craemer at work in her coastal Delaware studio. "There is nothing difficult about making feet," she says. "It's a matter of breaking it down into its components and having the patience to do each little step. You have to take the time to think about it as you do it and not rush through it."

About the Author

Curtis Badger has written widely about wildfowl art, wildfowl hunting, and conservation issues in general. His articles have appeared in many national and regional magazines, and he serves as editor of *Wildfowl Art Journal,* which is published by the Ward Foundation. He is currently working with carver Jim Sprankle on a book on wildfowl painting techniques, and he is writing a book about growing up on the Virginia coast. He lives in Onley, Virginia.

Other Books of Interest to Bird Carvers

Bird Carving Basics: Eyes
A wide variety of techniques for creating all kinds of wildfowl eyes.
by Curtis J. Badger

How to Carve Wildfowl
The masterful techniques of nine international blue-ribbon winners.
By Roger Schroeder

How to Carve Wildfowl Book 2
Features eight more master carvers and the tools, paints, woods, and techniques they use for their best-in-show carvings.
By Roger Schroeder

Waterfowl Carving with J. D. Sprankle
A fully illustrated reference to carving and painting 25 decorative ducks.
by Roger Schroeder and James D. Sprankle

Making Decoys the Century-Old Way
Detailed, step-by-step instructions on hand-making the simple ye coys of yesteryear.
By Grayson Chesser and Curtis J. Badger

How to Paint Songbirds
How to Paint Shorebirds
How to Paint Owls
How to Paint Gamebirds
Watercolor, gouache, and acrylic techniques, beautiful color sequ ing instructions show how to add life to bird paintings on any surf
by David Mohrhardt

John Scheeler, Bird Carver
A tribute to the bird-carving world's master of masters, John Sch
by Roger Schroeder

Carving Miniature Wildfowl with Robert Guge
Scale drawings, step-by-step photographs and painting keys der that make Guge's miniatures the best in the world.
by Roger Schroeder and Robert Guge

Songbird Carving with Ernest Muehlmatt
Muehlmatt shares his expertise on painting, washes, feather flicking, and burning, plus insights on composition, design, proportion, and balance.
by Roger Schroeder and Ernest Muehlmatt

For complete ordering information, write:
Stackpole Books
P.O. Box 1831
Harrisburg, PA 17105
or call 1-800-READ-NOW